POETRY FROM STRATA FLORIDA

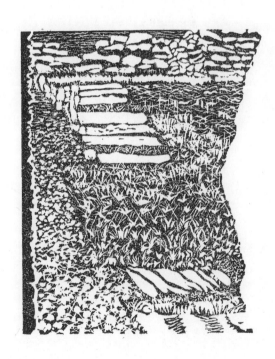

i

ALSO BY MARTIN LOCOCK

Prose

THE FLOW OF THOUGHT: A MANAGER'S GUIDE TO
USING POETRY FOR REFLECTION
(Carreg Ffylfan Press, 2010)

10 SIMPLE STEPS TO BETTER ARCHAEOLOGICAL
MANAGEMENT: PRACTICAL ADVICE FOR PROJECT
MANAGERS TO IMPROVE THEIR PERFORMANCE
(Carreg Ffylfan Press, 2012)

(editor)
MEANINGFUL ARCHITECTURE: SOCIAL
INTERPRETATIONS OF BUILDINGS
(Avebury Press, 1994)

Poetry

CAREFULLY CHOSEN WORDS
(Carreg Ffylfan Press, 2010)

TRAVELS WITH A NOTEBOOK
(Carreg Ffylfan Press, 2011)

REMOVALS
(Carreg Ffylfan Press, 2012)

POETRY FROM STRATA FLORIDA

AN ANTHOLOGY OF WORK INSPIRED BY THE YSTRAD FFLUR LANDSCAPE, 1350-2013

edited by
MARTIN LOCOCK

illustrated by
Linden Fletcher

photography by
Scott Waby

2nd impression

The right of Martin Locock to be identified as the creator of this work has been asserted in accordance with sections 77 and 79 of the Copyright, Designs and Patents Act 1988.

Published by
Carreg Ffylfan Press
38 New Road, Gwaun Cae Gurwen, Ammanford,
Carmarthenshire, UK SA18 1UN
www.carregffylfan.co.uk
carregffyflan@gmail.com

ISBN 978-0-9565067-5-7

Printed in Great Britain by Lulu.com

Contents

Introduction   1

Part 1

Dafydd ap Gwilym Mis Mai a Mis Tachwedd
    (May and November)   12

Grufudd Gryg I'r ywen uwchben bedd Dafydd ap
    Gwilym (To the yew above the grave of
    Dafydd ap Gwilym)   16

Guto'r Glyn Salwch yr Abad Rhys ap Dafydd o
    Ystrad-fflur (The illness of Abbot Rhys ap
    Dafydd of Strata Florida)   20

Dafydd Nanmor Abaty Ystrad Fflur pan
    atgyweiriwyd ef gan yr Abad Morgan
    (Strata Florida restored by Abbot Morgan)   26

T Gwynn Jones Ystrad Fflur (Strata Florida)   32

Hedd Wyn Ystrad Fflur (Strata Florida)   34

R S Thomas Ystrad Fflur (Strata Florida)   74

Harri Webb Thanks in Winter   76

Ruth Bidgood At Strata Florida   78

Moelwyn Merchant Dafydd lies at Ystrad Fflur   80

Gillian Clarke At Ystrad Fflur   90

Gillian Clarke Dyddgu replies to Dafydd   92

Caroline Gill 1st May: Red Kite at Strata Florida   94

Byron Beynon Ystrad Fflur   95

Gwyneth Lewis Ystrad Fflur   96

Gwyneth Lewis Strata Florida   97

Part 2   100
Martin Locock Scribe and Scripture

Martin Locock Gorffwysfa (Resting place for   101
    Dafydd ap Gwilym) (Gorffwysfa Dafydd ap
    Gwilym)
Kathy Miles The Creed of Cataloguing   102
Carol Manwell Scriptorium   104
Sue Moules The Pilgrim   105
Sue Moules The Taliesin Stone   106
Anthony Kendrew Strata Florida   108
Amanda Pickering Cyfeillgarwch (Friendship)   110
Mary Overton Benediction   112
Josie Smith Strata Florida   113

Contributors   115
Acknowledgements   121

from Hugh Hughes, *The Beauties of Cambria* (1823)

INTRODUCTION

Visitors to Strata Florida often remark that it seems a special place. What they consider to constitute this specialness varies - some feel it is the natural beauty, some its mythic and historical associations, and some its tranquility or holiness. Poets tend to perceive this specialness as inspiration. Often a visit is described as a 'pilgrimage', even where there is no spiritual intent.

The most obvious feature of Strata Florida to the modern visitor is its seclusion - at the end of the short valley cutting into the western shoulder of the Cambrian Mountains, it is a long way from anywhere. Even from Llangurig, Aberystwyth or Lampeter it is a lengthy winding journey through rugged and rocky terrain. Unlike the urban bustle of Neath and Margam Abbeys, or the tourist throngs of Tintern, Strata Florida encourages reflection and retreat.

Many poets have found inspiration in the place and its associations, but this inspiration has followed many different paths. The figure of Dafydd ap Gwilym, standing both as a real individual and as a hero-poet or Welsh icon, has often featured in dialogue with the poet's imagination, while other recurrent themes include the Gothic ruins and their monastic creators, the rivers, trees and moorlands, the absence of human company and the presence of wildlife, particularly the now-emblematic Red Kites that haunt the skies. Strata Florida continues to offer strands of meaning to successive generations of poets.

"The house on the bank of the blue Teifi", 1164-1539

The Cistercian abbey of Strata Florida was founded by the Norman lord Robert FitzStephen in 1164, at a site between Tregaron and Pontrhydfendigaid on the east bank of Cors Caron bog in the eastern part of modern Ceredigion. The monks had come from Whitland Abbey in Pembrokeshire. The abbey took its Welsh name, Ystrad Fflur, from the river Fflur on whose banks it sits (*ystrad* meaning plain, *fflur* flowers), transformed into the Latin form of Strata Florida.

A few years later, Lord Rhys, Prince of Deheubarth, had regained control of Ceredigion, and the abbey was re-founded on its present site, between the rivers Teifi and Glasffrwd in the shadow of the Cambrian Mountains. The abbey was granted extensive lands, making it an important secular power as well as a spiritual and cultural centre.

In a Cistercian abbey, the choir monks were confined mainly to the cloister and the church, their lives governed by the regular pattern of saying Mass interspersed with work, including the making and copying of manuscripts. The abbey had taken over responsibility for maintaining the Brut y Tywysogion, annals of the princes, and their copies of gospels and Mabinogion stories circulated widely. The *conversi* (lay brothers) spent much of their time working on the abbey's lands. The abbot oversaw the institution and formed part of the social elite of medieval Wales. (The life of Cistercians in Wales is the subject of the recent volume *Monastic Wales* (Burton & Stober 2013), and the history of abbey has been summarized by Williams (2012)).

2

With its close links with the princes of Deheubarth, whose main royal centre was Dinefwr Castle, Carmarthenshire, the fortunes of the abbey closely tracked those of the independent Welsh princedoms in their conflicts with the Norman lords and English kings. Thus in the first hundred years of its foundation it flourished, reaching a zenith in 1238 when Llywelyn Fawr, prince of Gwynedd, summoned the Welsh princes to the abbey to solemnly swear fealty to his successor. In the aftermath of Edward I's conquest of Wales in 1277-1284, Deheubarth became an English vassal and in the subsequent revolts the abbey repeatedly suffered, with English troops quartered in its buildings and a series of fires; on several occasions the Abbey successfully sought exemption from making payments to the motherhouse of Cîteaux because of the poor state of its finances. The abbey continued to be a place of pilgrimage, but by the early 16th century the number of monks had shrunk to eight.

In 1536 John Leland visited the Abbey:

> The church of Strata Florida is large, side aisled and cross aisled. By it is a large cloister, the fratery and infirmary be now mere ruins. The cemetery wherein the country about doth bury is very large, and meanly walled with stone. In it be 39 great yew trees. The base court or camp afore the abbey is very fair and large. The foundation of the body of the church was made to have been 60 foot longer than it is now.

Thus the final closure of the Abbey by Henry VIII in 1539 put an end to a declining institution, and its library of manuscripts was dispersed.

"A roofless minster", 1540-2013

The lands of the Abbey were held briefly by the Crown before being sold to the Stedman family, who established a new secular estate, constructing a gentry house, Mynachlog Fawr, on the foundations of the Abbey's refectory. The surrounding area was laid out with avenues of trees, and a new gatehouse and buildings, but the Abbey church was left alone, as a roofless ruin. Burials continued in the graveyard and a chapel was built to serve the parish.

The Stedmans' estate later merged with the Trawsgoed estate of the Vaughan family, later Earls of Lisburne, centred on Nant-yr-Eos house. Mynachlog Fawr, no longer a gentry seat, became a tenant farm. In the mid 19th century an impressive group of farm buildings (a barn, cowshed and coach-house) were added, re-using window details from the abbey ruins.

The prosaic working farm continued alongside the increasingly-popular ruins. By the end of the 18th century a visit to Strata Florida was part of the itinerary of travellers to Wales, its Gothic prospect of nature conquering the fruit of human ambition offering a moral lesson on the temporary nature of all life. In 1847 the Dean of Hereford made the first archaeological excavation in the abbey. In the 1880s the engineer Stephen Williams came to the area to survey a proposed Aberystwyth-Rhayader railway line. He was a keen antiquarian and saw the potential of the Abbey as a tourist attraction. He persuaded the Cambrian Archaeological Association to fund the excavation and clearance of the ruins, and although the excavation techniques would not meet modern standards, the prompt and full publication of the report on the work established it as one of the most significant in medieval Wales.

George Eyre Evans, a local antiquarian, described the site in 1903:

> Two walks which none should miss are hence [Strata Florida abbey] to Pant-y-Fedwen through Glasffrwd Vale; and hence up the mountains to Teify lakes, source of the salmon noted River Teify. For the first of these turn sharp right at the gate of the Abbey Church and follow the lane as it wends its way up the valley, with Glasffrwd, i.e. Blue Brook – babbling over its rocky course, on the right. Here you are at once in the heart of the country:--
>
> *"Alone with the Alone"*
>
> sky, water, mountains, trees, rocks and birds. The monks knew well the value of this spot, here were – nay, still are, their wells of healing waters, -- iron, sulphur, chalybeate – used with benefit by the natives today. What more truly romantic spot can be imagined or desired than that round "Ffynnon dyffryn tawel," the "well of the silent grove"? Here, almost at the entrance to the cherry tree avenue of Pant y Fedwen – Birch grove – its cool waters still

bubble forth, much as they did when pilgrims to the Abbey slacked their thirst at its welcome brink.

The prosaic historical, architectural and archaeological narratives of the site are interwoven with the language and themes of Romantic literature and fanciful conjecture.

In 1919 the site was protected as a Scheduled Ancient Monument and in 1931 it was taken into Guardianship, managed by the Ministry of Works and latterly by Cadw: Welsh Historic Monuments. After improvements to the visitor centre in 2012 Cadw commissioned Gwyneth Lewis to write English and Welsh poems about the Abbey, which were then incorporated into artworks by Rob Turner.

"By Dafydd's grave in Ystrad Fflur"

In medieval times, poets were frequent visitors to Strata Florida Abbey, which was at the centre of cultural and linguistic Wales. The court poets composed praise poems for their patrons in the complex and sophisticated verse of the *cynghanedd*. The core of this form is syllable-counted lines, the repetition of patterns of consonants and the variation of vowels. Dafydd ap Gwilym (c. 1315 - c. 1350) was recognised as its master. He had strong links with Strata Florida and may have been buried there: as his friend Grufudd Gryg (c. 1310 - c. 1380) suggests in his poem, a yew tree in the churchyard may mark its location. The abbots were important temporal powers and Guto'r Glyn (c. 1412 - c. 1493) and Dafydd

Nanmor (c. 1450 - c. 1490) were commissioned by successive abbots to write poems.

The cultural significance of Strata Florida in 19th century Wales is reflected in its emergence as a subject for poetry. In 1916 the National Eisteddfod was held at Aberystwyth and the subject for the competition for the chair was an *awdl* on Ystrad Fflur. The chair was won by John Ellis Williams, but Hedd Wyn also competed (he was to win the chair posthumously the following year). T. Gwynn Jones wrote a short poem in Welsh, published in 1934, and an English translation appeared in Keydrich Rhys' magazine *Wales* in 1945.

Harri Webb visited Ystrad Fflur in 1965 on the day of T. S. Eliot's death, and wrote the poem "Thanks in winter", and was followed by Ruth Bidgood, Moelwyn Merchant, Gillian Clarke and R. S. Thomas. Each poet responded directly to the location - there little indication that they were responding to earlier works, although Gwyneth Lewis was familiar with T. Gwynn Jones' poem.

This volume contains every poem about Strata Florida that could be traced with the exception of that by John Ellis Williams and John Ormond's "Lament for a leg", inspired by the gravestone in St Mary's churchyard recording the burial of a severed leg there following an accident. The victim later emigrated and died abroad, so was not re-united with his appendage.

The final part of the volume comprises contributions from Lampeter Writers Workshop. This group was founded in 1984, when Gillian Clarke was a creative writing fellow at St David's University College Lampeter; Gillian invited local writers to meet and the group's first members, Sue Moules, Kathy Miles and Andrew Hassam joined her. The group is said to be longest-running weekly writers' group in Wales, and still meets during term time in what is now the University of Wales Trinity Saint David, and has produced three anthologies: *The Writing Room*, *To the Edge of the Page*, and *A Star fell from Orion*.

Part of each meeting is dedicated to poems written for a theme, and following the Celtic myth and landscape conference at Lampeter in 2012, Strata Florida was selected. The idea of an anthology bringing together the medieval and later poems about the Abbey also arose during a rainswept and thoughtful tour of the ruins as part of the conference. Members of the Group have recently adopted the name Red Heron for public readings and events.

Translations

The medieval Welsh texts, and Hedd Wyn's poem are presented in parallel with a literal English translation, without an attempt to replicate the complex metre of the original. Edwin Stanley James' translation of T Gwynn Jones follows closely both its meaning and rhyme scheme. Gwyneth Lewis has written separate English and Welsh poems rather than two versions of one poem, and Martin Locock's versions of Gorffwysfa vary slightly in meaning as well as language.

Details of the contributors, sources and acknowledgments will be found at the end of the volume (p. 115)

References and further reading

Burton, J & Stober, K. (ed.) 2013 *Monastic Wales, New Approaches* (University of Wales Press, Cardiff)

Evans, G. E. 1904 *Cardiganshire: a personal survey of some of its antiquities, chapels, churches, fonts, plate and registers* (Aberystwyth)

Gramich, K. 2003 "Mirror games: Self and (M)Other in the poetry of R. S. Thomas", in D. W. Davies (ed.) *Echoes to the Amen: Essays after R. S. Thomas* (University of Wales Press, Cardiff)

Jarvis, M. 2008 *Welsh Environments in Contemporary Poetry* (University of Wales Press, Cardiff)

Miall, D. S. 2000 "Locating Wordsworth: "Tintern Abbey" and the community with nature", *Romanticism on the Net* **20**
[from www.erudit.prg/revue/ron/2000/v/n20/005949ar.html accessed 18 March 2013]

Morris, B. 1993 *Harri Web* (University of Wales Press, Cardiff)

Ward, J. P. 2001 *The Poetry of R. S. Thomas* (Seren, Bridgend)

Williams, D. H. 2010, 'The Cistercians in West Wales II: Ceredigion', *Archaeologia Cambrensis* **159**, 241-286.

Part 1

DAFYDD AP GWILYM

Mis Mai a Mis Tachwedd

Hawddamor, glwysgor glasgoed,
Fis Mai haf, canys mau hoed,
Cadarn farchog, serchog sâl,
Cadwynwyrdd feistr coed anial,
Cyfaill cariad ac adar,
Cof y serchogion a'u câr,
Cennad nawugain cynnadl,
Caredig urddedig ddadl.
Mawr a fudd, myn Mair, ei fod,
Mai, fis difai, yn dyfod
Ar fryd arddelw, frwd urddas,
Yn goresgyn pob glyn glas.
Gwasgod praff, gwisgad priffyrdd,
Gwisgai bob lle â'i we wyrdd.
Pan ddêl yn ôl rhyfel rhew,
Pill doldir, pall adeildew –
Digrif fydd, mau grefydd grill,
Llwybr obry lle bu'r Ebrill –
Y daw ar uchaf blaen dâr
Caniadau cywion adar,
A chog ar fan pob rhandir,
A chethlydd a hoywddydd hir,
A nïwl gwyn yn ael gwynt
Yn diffryd canol dyffrynt,
Ac wybren loyw hoyw brynhawn,
A glaswydd aml a glwyswawn,

DAFYDD AP GWILYM (trans. Dafydd Johnston)

May and November

Hail to thee, fair chancel of the greenwood,
summer month of May, since it is this I long for,
mighty knight, lover's boon,
green-chained master of the wild forests,
companion of love and birds,
memory of lovers and their friend,
messenger of ninescore trysts,
affectionate and dignified meeting.
It is most beneficial, by Mary, that he,
May, faultless month, is coming
intent on claiming, warm dignity,
conquering every green vale.
Thick mantle, clothing of highways,
he would dress every place with his green fabric.
When he comes after the war of ice,
meadow's fortress, thickly woven garment –
pleasant will be the path below
where April was (birdsong is my worship) –
then songs of young birds
will come upon oak tops,
and a cuckoo on every region's height,
and a songbird and long fine days,
and white mist before the wind
shielding the middle of a valley,
and bright sky on a fine afternoon,
and many green trees and fair gossamer,

Ac adar aml ar goedydd,
Ac irddail ar wiail wŷdd,
A chof fydd Forfudd f'eurferch,
A chyffro saith nawtro serch.

Annhebig i'r mis dig du
A gerydd i bawb garu,
A bair tristlaw a byrddydd
A gwynt i ysbeilio gwŷdd,
A llesgedd, breuoledd braw,
A llaesglog a chenllysglaw,
Ac annog llanw ac annwyd,
Ac mewn naint llifeiriaint llwyd,
A dwyn sôn mewn afonydd,
A llidio a duo dydd,
Ac awyr drymled ledoer
A'i lliw yn gorchuddio'r lloer.
Dêl iddo, rhyw addo rhwydd,
Deuddrwg am ei wladeiddrwydd.

and many birds on trees,
and fresh leaves on branches of trees,
and Morfudd my bright girl will be in mind,
and the thrill of all the escapades of love.
[May is] nothing like the nasty black month
which forbids everyone from making love,
which causes grim rain and short days
and wind to strip the trees,
and sluggishness, dreadful frailty,
and a trailing cloak and hail,
and incites floods and cold
and brown torrents in streams,
and roaring in rivers,
and daylight inflamed and darkening,
and a heavy cold sky
whose colour blots out the moon.
May he suffer (easy sort of threat)
two misfortunes for his discourtesy.

GRUFFUDD GRYG

I'r ywen uwchben bedd Dafydd ap Gwilym

Yr ywen i oreuwas
Ger mur Ystrad-fflur a'i phlas,
Da Duw wrthyd, gwynfyd gwŷdd,
Dy dyfu yn dŷ Dafydd.
Dafydd Llwyd a'th broffwydawdd
Er cyn dy dyfu rhag cawdd;
Dafydd, gwedi dy dyfu,
A'th wnaeth, o'i fabolaeth fu,
Dy urddo, yn dŷ irddail,
Tŷ â phob llwyn yn dwyn dail;
Castell cudd meirw rhag eirwynt
Cystal â'r pren gwial gynt;
Dy leau bu deuluaidd,
Dy wrysg, dy gangau, dy wraidd.

Mae danad ym mudaniaeth
Bedd rhwym, nid o'm bodd yr aeth,
Bydaf englynion bydoedd,
Bu ddewr ef, mewn bedd yr oedd,
A synnwyr cerdd a synnud,
A gwae Ddyddgu pan fu fud,
Gwnaeth ei theuluwas lasryw
I'w hael dyfu tra bu byw;
Gwna dithau, geiniau dethol,
Gywirder i Nêr yn ôl.
Addfwyn warchadw ei wyddfa,
Drybedd yw, fodrabaidd dda.

GRUFFUDD GRYG (trans. Dafydd Johnston)

To the Yew-tree above Dafydd ap Gwilym's Grave

The yew-tree for the best young man
by the wall of Strata Florida and its mansion,
God's blessing on you, paradise of trees,
that you have grown to be Dafydd's house.
Dafydd Llwyd prophesied before you grew
that you would be a shelter against affliction;
after you grew Dafydd from his youth onwards
exalted you as a house of green leaves,
a dwelling with leaves on every bush;
a castle shielding the dead from icy wind,
as good as the tree from the saplings long ago;
your locations were dignified,
your foliage, your branches, your roots.

Beneath you in the silence
of the sealed grave (he went there against my
        wishes)
is he who was the hive of all the world's *englynion*,
he was fearless, he was in a grave,
and you felt the sense of song,
and woe to Dyddgu when he fell silent.
Her young minstrel glorified
his mistress while he lived.
May you now with your fine branches
serve the Lord faithfully in return.
Protect his tomb tenderly,
good matronly yew like a three-footed pot.

Na ddos gam, na ddysg omedd,
Ywen, odduwch ben y bedd.
Geifre ni'th lwgr nac afrad
Dy dwf yng ngwendre' dy dad.
Ni'th lysg tân, anian annerch,
Ni thyr saer, ni'th ddyfriw serch;
Ni'th bilia crydd, mewn dydd dyn,
Dy dudded yn dy dyddyn;
Ni'th dyr hefyd, rhag bryd braw,
Â bwyell rhag ei bwyaw
(Ir dy faich i ar dy fôn)
Taeog na chynuteion.
Dail yw'r to, da le yw'r tau,
Diwartho Duw dy wyrthiau.

Do not go a single step, yew-tree,
from above the grave, stick to your post.
Goats will not despoil you
and your growth is not wasted in your father's fine
        home.
Fire will not burn you, courteous nature,
no carpenter will cut you, love will not wound you;
no cobbler will ever peel off
your cloak in your house;
nor will any churl or wood-gatherers
break you with an axe lest they be beaten,
have no fear,
green is the load on your trunk.
Leaves are your covering, your place is a good one,
may God glorify your marvellous properties.

GUTO'R GLYN

Salwch yr Abad Rhys ap Dafydd o Ystrad-fflur

Arglwydd Rys, eryr gwleddrym,
Abad wyd a bywyd ym,
A phriffordd cerdd a'i phroffwyd,
A philer aur teml Fflur wyd.
Ai gwir dy fod yn gorwedd?
Os gwir, mau ysgar â medd.
Anhunawg, fy neheunaf,
Ydiw dy glêr od wyd glaf.
Digiaw yr wyf, deg ei rudd,
Dyfr gost, am dy fawr gystudd.
Dy glefyd, fy niwyd nêr,
Yn Actwn yw fy nicter.
Er na bwyf â'r awen bur
I'th ddilid – dos o'th ddolur –
F'uchenaid tra fych yno
A drig yn edrych dy dro.
Diriaid fûm am dy orwedd,
Dagrau byth a'm dwg i'r bedd.
Oer yw hon, gledr dwyfron glos,
Rhag ofn fal rhew gaeafnos,
A chul gan fynych wylaw
Y grudd gwlyb a gurawdd glaw.

Ar dduw Mawrth yr oeddem wŷr,
A'th farwchwedl a ddoeth Ferchyr.
Dengyn y ceisiawdd d'angau
Dy ddwyn yn y dydd dduw Iau.

GUTO'R GLYN (trans. Dafydd Johnston)

The illness of Abbot Rhys ap Dafydd of Strata Florida

Lord Rhys, eagle of abundant feasts,
you are abbot and life to me,
and the main road of song and its prophet,
and you are the golden pillar of the church of Fflur.
Is it true that you are ill?
If it is true, then I will be deprived of mead.
Your poets are sleepless
if you are ill, my dexterous lord.
I am grieving because of your great disease,
expense of waters, fair-cheeked one.
Your sickness in Acton
is the cause of my grief, my true lord.
Although I do not follow you there
with the pure muse – cast off your illness –
my sigh will stay
to see how you are whilst you are there.
I have been wretched because of your illness,
ceaseless tears are taking me to the grave.
This tight breast is cold
like ice on a winter night because of fear,
and the wet cheek beaten by rain
is wasted by frequent weeping.

We were contented men on Tuesday,
and news of your decease came on Wednesday.
Grimly did your death try
to carry you off during the day on Thursday.

Deufwy oedd lef y dref draw
Duw Gwener yn dy gwynaw.
Duw Sadwrn cathl dwys ydoedd,
Diriaid o beth drwy dyb oedd.
Duw Sul chwedlau da y sydd,
Duw Llun y daw llewenydd.

Costia, Rhys, cais adaw'r haint,
Cyfod wrth wyn y cwfaint.
Na chythrudd y ddeurudd wych,
N'ad ddaly arnad ddolurnych.
Oni fynny ynn, f'annwyl,
Ellwng pawb fal llong eb hwyl,
Och f'arglwydd, iach o fawrglwyf
Fyddy Rys. Rhyfeddu'r wyf,
O baud glaf, hoywnaf hynod,
Na bai glaf wyneb y glod.

Rhys, ni'th orfuwyd er hawl
Abadau neu wŷr bydawl.
Aeth hawlwyr gynt i'th ddilyn,
Ofer, fy hoywner, fu hyn.
Oferach oedd i fawrlal
Geisiaw diswyddaw dy sâl.
Ni wrth-wynebawdd, fy naf,
Neb yt, Rys, na baud drawsaf.
Am hyn gwybydd, fy mhiniwn,
Orfod yr haint oerfudr hwn.

The cry of the town yonder was twice as great
lamenting you on Friday.
On Saturday there was a sombre song,
it was thought to be a wretched matter.
On Sunday the news is good,
on Monday joy will come.

Spend, Rhys, seek to get rid of the disease,
rise up to the delight of the monks.
Don't pain the lovely cheeks,
don't let wasting sickness take hold of you.

Unless you want us all, my dear one,
to be set loose like a ship without a sail,
oh my lord, you will get well
from great sickness Rhys. I am amazed,
if you are ill, lovely excellent lord,
that the face of praise is not ill too.

Rhys, no one has ever got the better of you
despite the claims of abbots or laymen.
Claimants did pursue you once,
it was in vain, my fine lord.
It was even more vain for great Yale
to try to deprive you of the profit of your office.
You have always been stronger,
Rhys my lord, than anyone who ever opposed you.
Because of that, this is my opinion,
make sure that you defeat this horrible disease.

Dod o'i swydd, dy wawdwas wyf,
Dial, arglwydd, dy lwyrglwyf.
Ti a gai, erfai arfoll,
Arfau Duw i'w orfod oll.

Bellach bydd iach o'm bodd i,
Bened ni'th ad i boeni.
Boni'th wna, bennaeth neiaint,
Berned deg eb arnad haint,
Dy wlad a rydd, dielw dranc,
Da i Dduw er dy ddianc.
Di-brid fo ym dy bryder,
Dros dy glwyf mae'n drist y glêr.
Dy boen dwg mewn diben da,
Doi i'th bwynt, Duw a'th beintia.
Dolur a'th wnaeth yn gaethach,
Duw a'th wnêl dithau yn iach.

Put it out of office, I am your poetic servant,
avenge, lord, all your malady.
You will have the weapons of God
in order to defeat it completely, splendid promise.

Henceforth be well as I wish,
St Benedict will not let you suffer.
If fair St Bernard does not rid you
of your disease, leader of nephews,
the people of your region will give payment
to God in order to free you (your death would cause
        loss).
May concern about you not be costly for me,
the poets are sad because of your malady.
Bring your sickness to a good conclusion,
you will get well, God will colour you.
Illness has made you captive,
may God make you well again.

DAFYDD NANMOR

**Abaty Ystrad Fflur pan atgyweiriwyd ef gan yr
Abad Morgan**

Y tŷ o lan Teifi las,
Wyth ugeinporth i'th gwmpas,
Y mae gair am ei gweiriaw
I Forgan dros Fyrgwyn draw.
Y côr, efô a'i cweiriawdd
Â dorau teg o wydr tawdd.
Aeth hanner gwerth ei hynys
I wydro hwn wedi Rhys.
Ystrad-fflur ar waith curas,
A gynau plwm i gan plas.
Lliw'r gynau oll rhyg Ionawr,
Lliw dŵr marl fal llwydrew mawr.
Ar ei chôr llawer toriad
Ar fainc côr Rhufain y'i cad.
Teg yw sŵn byrdwn lle bo,
Trebl a mên trwy blwm yno.

Pe bai'n fil, pawb yn ei fedd,
Feirw yn hon o frenhinedd,
Y mae rhwng ei muriau hi
Erw i gladdu arglwyddi.
Gwisgwyd oll, gwisg hyd allawr,
Gweau plwm am gyplau mawr.
O ugain we ei gŵn haf,
O gan gwe ei gŵn gaeaf.
Y gweoedd hyn, a'i gwŷdd hi,
Forgan, sydd frigawns iddi.

DAFYDD NANMOR (trans. Dafydd Johnston)

Strata Florida restored by Abbot Morgan (*c.* 1450)

The house on the bank of the blue Teifi,
with eight-score gates around you,
Morgan is famed as far as Burgundy
for having restored it.
He restored the choir
with fair doors of molten glass.
Half the wealth of the island
went to glass this house after Rhys.
Strata Florida decorated like a cuirass,
with gowns of lead enough for a hundred palaces.
The gowns are all the colour of January rye,
the colour of lime water like a great frost.
On its choir is many a carving
such as those on Rome's choir.
Lovely is the sound of the refrain,
treble and mean through lead there.

If there were a thousand kings
all dead in their graves here,
there is between these walls
an acre to bury lords.
Leaden webs have been woven
as far as the altar about great beams.
Its summer gown is twenty webs,
and its winter gown is one hundred.
These webs and its wood,
Morgan, are like a coat of mail on the church.

Un dydd ni rifwn o'i dôr
Ei deri oll hyd yr allor.
Ergyd saeth o dderwgoed serth
Yw ei chrib uwch yr aberth.
Mae derw yrhôm a dwyrain,
Rif myrdd ar fwäau main.

Er ei gost wrth wŷr a gwaith
A cheginau chweugeinwaith,
Ni bu air, mwy no barwn,
Am leihau saig ym mhlas hwn.
Mwy no'i glych ni mynnai glos
Na neuaddau'n anniddos.
Clochdy mawr, calchaid, mawrwyn,
Cort o'r gwaith, caer y Tŵr Gwyn.
Pwy a edrych bob Hydref
Golwg uwch no'i geiliog ef?
Pan fu'r dŵr ugain hwryd,
Heb un bont, uwchben y byd,
Gallai hwn i ar gerrig lliw
Gadw y delwau rhag dilyw.

Toau a phlwm trwm, tramawr,
Tŷ deri maint Tewdwr Mawr.
To ar wŷdd, ni ad trwyddaw
Rew na gwlyb nac eiry na glaw.

I could not count in a single day
all its oak beams from door to altar.
Its crest rises as far as an arrow shot
in towering oak above the host.
There are a myriad of oaktrees
on stone arches between us and the east.

Despite his expense on men and work
and kitchens by the score,
it has never been said, any more than a baron,
that a dish was stinted in this man's house.
He would have no cloister, no more than his bells,
nor halls which were not weather-tight.
A great whitewashed belltower,
built like a court, the White Tower's stronghold.
Who looks higher every autumn
than his weather-cock?
When the water was twenty fathoms deep
over the world without any bridge,
on coloured stones he could keep
the effigies out of the flood.

Roofs with great thick lead,
an oaken house as big as that of Tewdwr Mawr.
A roof on trees, it won't let through
ice or moisture or snow or rain.

Mawr yw cost ar y mur cau
A'i gaer wydr a'i gaeredau;
Llu gaeredau'n cau rhag gwynt,
Lliw gaeredau Lloegr ydynt.

Gwedi caffo goed cyffion
I gwpláu holl gyplau hon,
Bo byw yno i bob ynys
Bedwar oed yr Abad Rys.

A glass fortress and square panes
have been put at great cost on its enclosing wall;
rows of panes shutting out the wind,
they are of one colour with England's stained glass.

When he has got enough tree trunks
to complete all the coupled beams of this church,
may he live there for all the world to see
four times as long as Abbot Rhys.

T. GWYNN JONES

Ystrad Fflur

Mae dail y coed yn Ystrad Fflur
Yn murmur yn yr awel,
A deuddeng Abad yn y gro
Yn huno yna'n dawel.

Ac yno, dan yr ywen brudd
Mae Dafydd ber ei gywydd
A llawer penaeth llym ei gledd
Yn ango'r bedd tragywydd.

Er bod yr haf pan ddel ei oed,
Yn deffro coed i ddeilio,
Ni ddeffry dyn, a gwaith ei llaw
Sy'n distaw ymddadfeilio.

Ond er mai angof angau prudd
Ar adfail ffydd a welaf,
Pan rodiwyf ddaear Ystrad Fflur
O'm dolur ymdawelaf.

T. GWYNN JONES (trans. Edwin Stanley James)

Ystrad Fflur

The voice of leaves in Ystrad Fflur
    Is clear upon the air,
And twelve dead Abbots buried deep
    In sleep are resting there.

And where the sombre yew-trees wave
    Ap Gwilym's grave was made,
And fighting men who dreamed of fame
    Without a name were laid.

Though Summer comes again to wake
    The brake to leaf and flower,
Man sleeps - while slowly fall
    Cornice and wall and tower.

But though oblivion wrought by death
    On ruined faith I see,
Yet in the pale of Ystrad Fflur
    My fear and sorrow flee.

HEDD WYN

Ystrad Fflur

I

A MI yng nghwmni dwsmel awelon
Yn rhodio ogylch bro Ceredigion,
Deriais wrth Ystrad dirion, -lle yr oedd
Ysbryd oesoedd annisbur a dwysion.
      Yno bu cwrdd wyneb certh
      Adfail hen neuadd brydferth
      Ac oed rhyw dywell bell bau
      Yn ymyrraeth â'i muriau.

Yn nydd ei llachar gynnar ogoniant,
Hi fu'n gynefin â gwae a nwyfiant;
Ei ffenestri, mal lliant - aml-liwiog,
O hud eurog a cherfiadau ariant;
      A thrwsiwyd prydferth ddrysi
      Lliwoedd haf i'w chelloedd hi;
      Cans gwedd fflwch ei harddwch oedd
      Yn sisial dyfais oesoedd.

Eurwawd organau y Brodyr Gwynion
Ohoni dorrai trwy'r Ystrad dirion,
A sŵn lleddf y clych meddfon - oedd yno
Fel su wylo ar felys awelon,
      Ac o'i chôr a'i hallor hi
      Deuai hirion baderi,
      A swynol ysgawn seiniau
      Ave hen trwy'i chain fwâu.

HEDD WYN (trans. Martin Locock)

Strata Florida

I

With the soft sweet winds
I walked the bounds of Ceredigion,
And came to gentle Ystrad,
where the spirit of the past was summoned
>There was met a wondrous sight
>Ruin of a fine old hall
>A far land's time
>has broken its walls.

In the day of its bright early glory,
Accustomed both to woe and strength;
Its windows, a multicoloured flood
From golden magic and costly sculptures
>The lovely thorns brought back
>Summer's colours to their cells;
>The form of its beauty whispers
>The dreams of ages.

The golden organ of the White Brothers
Sounds through Ystrad's lands
And the sad chime of the gentle bells
Like a murmur on the honeyed breeze
>And from the choir and altar
>Would come long prayers
>And the charming soft sounds of
>Old Ave Marias through its fair arches.

Rhai dewr a hoffus ar grwydr o draffell
A gyrchai yngo i gôr a changell;
A doi'r beirdd o'u hendre bell - dan ei nen,
Wroniaid awen bryd heldrin dywell;
     Ar ei phwys y gorffwysynt,
     Awenwyr ac arwyr gynt,-
     Diasgloff gewri disglair
     Caeth i swyn y Forwyn Fair.

O'i fyd di-wên doi aml unben tanbaid
Yno i degwch ei swyn bendigaid;
Ac yno deuai'r gweiniaid - o'u pell bau
I roi eu horiau i'r Wyry euraid.
     Er trymder yr amseroedd
     Ei byd syml darbodus oedd
     I'r clwyfus yn elusen
     A gwin i wŷr egwan hen.

Ac yno cedwid pob dysg odidog
A "rhuddem roddion" henfeirdd mawreddog;
Canys cai'r wlad ddrycinog - ynddi hi
Lên a dyri yn ei dydd blinderog.
     Synod wen! rhoes, yn ei dydd,
     Hafan i ddysg a chrefydd,
     Pan oedd rhyfel a'i helynt
     Yn gwasgu ar Gymru gynt.

Some bold and lovable man, enmeshed by troubles
Would approach choir and chancel;
And poets drawn here from their distant halls
Under this roof, where brave men muse on sad
matters
   Resting beside
   Past poets and former heroes
   Raising bright shouts
   To charm the Virgin Mary.

From a worldly life under some fiery lord
Charmed by a blessèd beauty;
And there came the weak from the farthest land
To give Virgin their golden hours.
   Through the sorrowed times
   A frugal life of thrift
   To give to the sick in charity
   And wine to the frail old man.

And there kept great knowledge
And bright ruby gifts of the old poets;
For those of the storm-blasted land
Literature and poetry for weary days.
   White Synod which gave in its day
   A home to learning and religion,
   When war's troubles
   Oppressed ancient Wales.

Y saint o'i mynwes wylies dreialon
A chur ein disegur dywysogion;
Erys ei Brut yr awron - fel crïau
Anniddig oriau a thrinoedd geirwon;
      Ei mynwes gadwes ar go
      Enwau dewrion diwyro,
      A'n cenedl glyw sŵn cyni
      Ei hen dras o'i chalendr hi.

Pand du fu dod o'r gelyn i rodio
Trwy oed a hinon yr Ystrad honno,
A gwelw adwyth i gludo - niwl di-hedd
Ar ei adanedd anhyfryd yno?
      Anhunedd ar ei hedd hi
      Dorres fel du bryderi;
      A chariai pob rhoch irad
      O'r ffriddoedd sŵn cymloedd cad.

Yno un hwyr 'roedd y deml yn eirias,
A'i meini henoed yn fflamio'n wynias;
Du y gofid a gafas - gan greulon
Gadau gelynion ac oed galanas.
      Yn nhawch hwyr ei myneich hi
      Wylai oed eu caledi,
      Heb allor na chôr na chân,-
      Oered a gloewod arian.

Its saints watched the trials
Of our pure and busy princes;
Preserved in the Brut - the hoarse cries
Of battle's troubled hours;
      Her bosom keeping the true
      brave and steadfast names,
      Hearing our nation's anguish
      In the old tale of its calendar.

A black band came from the enemy to roam
Through that age and to this Ystrad,
A pale evil to bring a mist of war
On its unlovely wings there
      Sleepless in her rest
      Breaking as a black doubt;
      Which carried all red waters
      From pastures loud with tumult.

One evening the heap was glowing
And its ancient flame lit the stones;
Black the sorrow - from cruel
Enemy armies and old blood price.
      In late haze her monks
      Saw an age of hardship,
      Without song or choir or altar, -
      Cold and moneyless.

Oriog helynt o alar ac wylo,
Yw trawd hanes trwy yr Ystrad honno,
Cans y gelyn ers cyn co' - megis bâr
Rhyw gyhwrdd anwar a gerddai yno.
      Iddo ef y neuadd oedd
      Yn dŷ gloddest a gwleddoedd;
      A charnau 'i feirch chwerwon fu
      Hyd laswyr huodl Iesu.

'Rôl llid a gofid fal chwyth gaeafau,
Tawodd y drin fin ei Sagrafennau;
Weithiau mae 'i hadfail hithau - 'n ddolurus
Gŵyn ar wefus holl wynt y canrifau;
      A thrig gwyll wrth ddorau cau
      Y byd oedd i'r abadau;
      Yntau dlws guwd o fwsog
      Melfed lle bu Cred y Grog.

II

Yng ngwyll oedais rhwng lledwyr
Dderi hen, a hedd yr hwyr
Hyd ddolydd mal oed ddiloes
Y byd aeth o wybod oes.

Yr owmal goed ymgrymynt
Ym mhryderi gweddi'r gwynt;
A'r lloer fel tröell arian
Ucho ar bwys breichiau'r ban.

40

Much trouble of grief and weeping,
Is the tale of Strata's history,
Since before the foe remembers -
Some savage walked there
   For him the hall was
   A banquet-house for feasting;
   And the bitter hooves of horses
   Trod the steps of Jesus.

After pain and distress as a harsh winter,
Silence fell on the Sacraments;
Sometimes the ruin itself would raise
Sore complaint in the wind's wail for centuries;
   Dusk remained when the doors closed
   The world of the abbots;
   Bright moss grows like velvet
   Where the Rood was holy.

II

In the twilight I lingered between twisted
Old oaks, and in the peace of evening
In meadows like a painless age
Passing from the known world.

The shining trees bowed
And prayed in the wind;
And the silver moon was a spinning wheel
Above cradling branches.

Doi isod nodau dwysion
Hen Garon deg arian dôn,
Maltae abad ym mhader
Yn llewych sant lluwch o sêr.

Gwelwn o'r parth darth yn don
Liw owmal ar Bumlumon;
A'i ridens cêl a chwelynt
Ar y gaer fel mynnai'r gwynt.

A thlysed gweled wedyn
Yn lleuer sant y lloer syn
Fryniau cain ar gywrain gyrch
Yng ngwynt yr eang entyrch;
A rhwng eu prydferth rengoedd
Erwau dwfn yr Ystrad oedd,
A llewych hir a mirain
Y lwys loer ar y las lain

Lle mae hi, fwyn Deifi deg,
O ryd i ryd yn rhedeg;
Yn y fro cofiai'r awen
Swyn actau sanct oesau hen,
Mal a wŷr yn hwyr ei oes
Ddewiniaeth gwawrddydd einioes;
Yna rhyngof a'r nennawr
Gwelwn dremyn murddyn mawr;
Yn y dud mor fud efô
A duw hen wedi huno

Below come the solemn notes
Of Old Garon's fair silver tone,
The chants of abbot and priest
In a glittered snowstorm of stars.

I saw a wave of mist
Cast enamel on Plynlimon;
Fringes of broom and heather
On the windswept fort.

And then see the beauty
In the holy moonlight
Elegant in a skilful haunt
Hills in the wide breathing sky;
And between their lovely ranks
Was Strata in the deep acres,
And long light glittering
Cold dew on a blue path

There she is, the fair maid Teifi,
From ford to ford running;
In the area remembered by the muse
Charmed by the acts of the old holy ages,
Like the men of later times
Witchcraft of the dawn of life;
Then between me and the heavens
I see the prospect of a great ruin;
In the darkness so silent
An old god sleeping

43

Mewn trymllyd adfyd ar ôl
Hen, hen feirwon anfarwol.

Yr adail lliw marwydos
Oedd yn un â'r bruddaidd nos;
Ei llaswyr oedd yr hwyrwynt
A'i gweddi oedd gweddi'r gwynt;
A lleisiau o bell oesoedd,
Fel atgof uwch angof, oedd
Yn fy enaid fy hunan,
Ac yn y gwynt ganai gân.
Tybiwn atsain o'r main mud
Rhyw bellter arab alltud,
Fal swyn ymeifl a synnwyr
O wylio hud gorwel hwyr;
Cans anneallt frud alltud
Oedd o fewn y neuadd fud.

Ac yno, fel bu ganwaith,
Rhoddwyd i mi freuddwyd maith,
A dyfod hyd i fyd oedd
Is y gŵys yng nghwsg oesoedd,
A chanfod iddo'n rhodio
Ŵr hen breg tros fryniau bro;
Yn ei gwfl y canai gwynt
Garol rhyw oes ddi gerrynt;
Wynned ei wisg amdano
Ag ewyn dŵr, neu 'i guawd o,
Ac ar ei ais gwelwn grog

In heaviness after adversity
Old, old rugged immortal.

The ember-toned fabric
Was one with gloomy night;
The rosary was the evening breeze
And its prayer was the prayer of the wind;
And voices of distant ages,
As higher memory forgotten, was
In my own soul,
And the wind sang a song.
I wonder in silence at the faint echo
Of some pleasant distant exile,
As charm and wisdom
From the magic of the dusk horizon;
Unearthly song of a rich stranger
Within the silent hall.

And there, as a hundred times before,
I fell into a deep dream,
A world that was coming up
Under the summons of a dormant age,
And find an old man strolling
Over the hills of the old country;
The wind sang in his hood
The song of some distant age;
White as his robes about him
As foam in water, or his flesh,
And I see hanging on his chest

Rwym o ruddaur mawreddog;
Ac yn ei law 'roedd cain lên
Ei dduwiol santaidd awen;
Eithr hyd erwau'r llathr diroedd
Ust rhyw ddwfn ddistawrwydd oedd.
Ar wyneb y mur yno
Y rhoddes drem hirddwys, dro;
Niwliog darth i'w lygaid oedd,
Lliw asur y pell oesoedd;
A didlawd y dywawd o
Er ei alar a'i wylo:

I'w rawd oer ban elo'r dydd
O lwyni'r Ystrad lonydd,
A'i gweld hi, deg leuad hwyr,
Ar ieuanc lwybrau'r awyr,
Hiraeth wêl, trwy'r gwynt melyn,
Ysbryd ag oes y Brawd Gwyn;
A'r llys fu'n gartre llaswyr
Liwir a gwawl oriog hwyr.

"O redyn y dyffryn dir
Eilwaith abadau elwir,
Ac eilwaith bydd tinc wylo
Rhyw osber hen ar draws bro;
Daw yr hen offerennau
O law'r bedd yn ôl i'r bau,
A llefair hud o'r gell frau
Felys araf laswyrau;
A'r myneich glân, tan ganu,

Grand golden binding;
And in his hand was fine lore
His pious holy muse;
As far as the acres of shining land
The hush was a deep silence.
To the face of the wall there
He turned his solemn gaze;
His eyes were fogged mist,
The azure of distant ages;
And was rich, it is said
Despite his grief and weeping:

To the cool peak the day comes
From the groves of Strata's lanes,
And see her, the fair late moon,
On her youthful orbit,
Homesick, through the yellow wind,
The spirit and the White Brother;
And the court that has been home of the rosary
Coloured by a speckled hedge.

"From the reeds of the valley
A second time the abbots called,
And again the chime sounded
For ancient Evensong across the lands;
Came the old masses
From the grave back to the soil,
And the magic words from the simple cell
Sweet slow rosary chants;
And the bright monks, singing

Gânt ddod, liw gwylanod lu,
O dyweirch y Cwm diwair
I oed â'r fwyn Forwyn Fair.

"A phan bo'r hwyr ar ffin bro
A nos-awel yn suo
Clywir sôn ysbrydion brud,
Is owmal darth, yn symud,
A diweirllu yn darllen
I ysig wŷr rhyw ddysg hen;
Eilwaith ceir gwylio helynt
Y dyddiau gwell, santaidd gynt,
A gweld mil seintiau diloes
Y byd aeth o wybod oes:
Rhodiant o'r bedd marwydos
Ar gaen niwl a lloergan nos.

"Eithr ar neshâd toriad dydd
Hwnt gwinau gant a gweunydd;
Hud yr hwyr o'r neuadd dry,
Ac oer fydd cainc y Wyry.
Y myneich dry'n goed maenol
A'r abadau'n darthiau dôl;
Try'r cannaid offeiriaid ffydd
Yn gawn wrth neint y gweunydd;
A'r deml freg dry'n gartre gwynt
A chethrin ysgrech uthrwynt;
A bydd curaw aflawen
Ar ei chôr a'i hallor hen."

They come, coloured like gulls,
From the mown turf of the Valley
For the sake of the Virgin Mary.

"And when it is late on the borders
A night-breeze murmured
The sound of ghosts was heard,
Under a shining mist, moving,
And a holy host reading
To wounded men of some past learning;
Once again can be seen
The better days, the ancient saints,
And see a thousand healed saints
Of a world passed from the age's knowledge:
They walk from the ashes of the grave
In the fresh fog and a moonlit night.

"But at the approach of daybreak
Across the hundred browning grasses;
The magic of the late hour leaves the hall
And the cold will spur the Virgin.
The monks become estate trees
And the abbots meadow mists;
Turns white priests
Into the reeds of the moor;
And the temple becomes the wind's home
And the cruel jay's haunt;
And the awful pain
At its ancient altar and choir. "

Ar hyn yr abad a drodd,
A'r caddug hwyr a'i cuddiodd;
Ac nid oedd ond cŵyn y dail
Hyd drofâu'r goetre fiwail
Unwedd y sant fwynaidd sôn
Ganai y Myneich Gwynion.

Yna mi a ddihunais,
Fel gwŷdd tan ddiofal gais
Addfwyn wynt, hithau'r feddf nos
Hyd dewddail y cwm diddos.

Eithr swyn nas traethai'r synnwyr
Oedd ar gêl awel yr hwyr
Fel mil gosberau diloes
Y byd aeth o wybod oes;
A drych syn y murddyn maith
Welwn fel mudan eilwaith.

III

Tramwyais yn hedd prim y boreddydd,
Fin Teifi donnog, wydrog, dafodrydd;
Ac yno daeth er gwên dydd - ysbryd oed
Rhyfelau henoed a gwŷr aflonydd.

    Eilwaith adfywiai dolur
    Ieuenctid hen actau dur;
    Ac yn y gwynt ganai gerdd
    Gwingai anniddig angerdd.

At this the abbot turned,
And the evening gloom hid him;
And there were only the restless leaves
Up past the turns of the forest path
Like the song of the Virgin saint
Sang by the White Monks.

Then I awoke,
Like the woods touched by
The gentle wind, chasing the shades of night
Up the leafy valley.

But the charm did not speak sense
On the cloistered evening breeze
As a thousand faint whispers
A world lost from the present age;
A mirror which sees the ruin
As silent again.

III

I passed in the dawn of the morning
The Teifi, undulating, glassy, whispering;
And there came the day's smile - the spirit of the age
Dreams of the elders and restless men.
     Renewing again the sorrow
     Youthful old deeds of steel;
     And the wind sang a poem
     Of writhing restless passion.

Yno tanodd gwelwn fynwent unig
A llewych hiraeth i'w thalaith helig;
A doi o ro y drymllyd drig - i'm bron
Nodau dwysion rhyw fudandod ysig;
  I'w herwau claf o hiraeth
  O'i boen hir aml unben aeth;
  A'r dewr o frad hir ei fro
  Ddihanges i'r bedd yngo.

Ar finion tyner y fynwent honno
Rhwng melyn redyn roedd macwy'n rhodio;
Heulog a dwfn ei lygaid o, - ac oed
Rhyw ddawn henoed yn eu gwyrdd yn huno.
  Yn ei drem 'roedd mwynder haf
  Ac enaid ar ei geinaf;
  Ac i'w lais islais glaslyn
  A threbl hesg wrth arab lyn.

Doedai a welir trwy goed y dolydd,
Doedai hanes ei dadau dihenydd,
Doedai a wŷr gwynt y dydd - a'r nifwl
Chwery ym mhannwl ac ochr y mynydd.
  Canys gwae y nosau gynt
  Erys yng nghôl y corwynt;
  A daw o'r hesg gyda'r hwyr
  Hanes tu hwnt i synnwyr.

Here below we see only the cemetery
A glittering longing for the sunlit lands;
And a roof-tile of the sultry sky- to my breast
Some silent summons rolled;
> To the patient plain of longing
> Its pain long ago gone;
> And the brave, betrayed, long from home
> Needless brought to grave close by.

On the soft limits of the churchyard
Between yellow ferns was a lord walking;
Bright and deep were his eyes, - and the age
Of some frail elder in their green sleep.
> In his gaze was a summer gentleness
> And his soul was fine;
> And his voice a cool undercurrent
> A pleasant treble of reeds in a lake.

Through the trees on the meadows,
Came the story of his ancient fathers,
Came the wind of the day - and the mist
Played in hollow and mountainside.
> For the woe of earlier nights
> Remains in the lap of the storm;
> A reed comes with twilight
> A history beyond sense.

Ac yna rhodiodd y macwy'n wridog
I hendref nychlyd, oer y fynachlog;
Ac ar ei llwydfur gwyrog - 'roedd esmwyth
Chwaon diadwyth a chân odidog.

    Oddi draw daeth torf lawen
    Ar ei thaith tua'r porth hen;
    Ar hyn y macwy a drodd,
    A di oed wrthi dwedodd:

"Mae rhyddid yr hen oesau mawreddog
Ban gerddai hedd trwy'r dudwedd odidog?
Mae y glew dramwyai glog, - a'r seintiau
Gerddai ar greigiau rhuddaur a grugog?

    Wele eu sorth achle sant
    Yn adfeilion difoliant,
    Mal duoer wedd teml dywell -
    Pantheon poen aethni pell.

"Ond cofia Teifi, ferch y gellïoedd,
Lymder eu hanes a'u gwenfflam drinoedd,
Canys fe chwardd drycinoedd-atgo 'u dig
Yng nghwm anniddig rhwng y mynyddoedd.

    Erys ar fin pob corwynt
    Oriog oes Ap Tewdwr gynt;
    A chân pob awel felys
    Lwydd a rhawd yr Arglwydd Rhys.

And then walked the lord, flushed
To the dusty hall, the cold monastery;
And on it chequered floors - there was an easy
Breath of wind and a magnificent song.
     There came forth a joyous crowd
     On its journey to the old gate;
     At this the lord turned,
     And ageless, said:

"Freedom of the grand old ages
When peace walked through this magnificent world
A valiant man crossed the stone, - and the saints
Walked on rusted rocks and heather
     Behold their fate to keep a saint
     In the forgotten ruins,
     The blackness of a dark temple -
     A pantheon of distant hurt.

"But remember Teifi, daughter of the groves,
The austerity of history and the battle flames,
Laughing at storms- memory of their anger
In the uneasy valley between the mountains.
     In every fickle tempest
     Was Ap Tewdwr before;
     And in the sweet song of every breeze
     Success and triumph of the Lord Rhys.

A'r dydd ar drywydd tros geyrydd gorwel
A cheinciau irwydd fel gwreichion cwrel,
I'r neuadd oer aml deyrn ddêl-o bell ddydd
Hendre ddihenydd rhyw diroedd anwel.
      Eilwaith y dewr Lywelyn,
      Ar ei rawd trwy'r erwau hyn,
      Dry gyda'i wŷr i gadw oed
      Yn llonydd y gell henoed.

Eithr pe cerddid brig yr ysig rosydd,
A'r corwynt yno yn curo'r ceyrydd,
Enaid wêl ddrych hefelydd - trem byddin
Erwin, a thrin ar fron a tharennydd,
      A bydd tros wyneb y bau
      Gynhyrfus gaen o arfau;
      A'r hoyw-wyr braisg, tarawan
      O'u gleifiau dig lif o dân.

Ac yna gwelir yr hen unbennau
O'u herwau breiniol yn ffoi i'r bryniau
O'r trinoedd a'r taranau,-athrist iaith
Neithior anobaith ar eu hwynebau:
      Eu gwlad o'u hôl fel ffagl dân
      Yn y duwch adawan;
      Yntau'r creulon estron ŵr
      Ogylch dry yn orchfygwr.

And the day came up over the forts on the horizon
And sparkled in the spruce like coral strands,
To the cold hall often tyrant-marred - from the
farthest days
A capital palace of some unseen lands.
>Again the brave Llywelyn,
>On patrol through these fields,
>With his men to keep
>The elderly safe in their cells.

But if I were to walk the summit's rolling plains,
And the wind there beat the forts,
My soul sees a matching mirror - a fierce army's eye
And battle on the breast and ridge
>And over the face of the country
>Renewed clashing of arms
>And the bold brave men, unleashing
>From their angry swords a stream of fire.

And then they see the old tyrants
Flee from the heroes to the hills
From wars and thunder, sorrowing
With the cast of despair on their faces:
>Their country behind them like a torch of fire
>In the darkness they left;
>He himself a brutal foreign man
>Turned conqueror.

Heddiw mae'r godidog dywysogion
Is y gaen isod yn cysgu'u noson;
Ond er enhuddo'r dewrion-bydd gofwy
Eu hanes hwy fyth ar grwydr y suon.
      Ac o'u teg feddau segur
      Rhyw hud fflam gaiff Ystrad Fflur
      A bydd ar awel y bau
      Hirfaith atsain eu harfau."

Yma y tawodd ei ymadroddion
A'u hud hwyliog, mal y tau awelon
O gaead frig coed y fron,-ar dorf aeth
I hyfryd hiraeth wrth gofio'r dewrion.
      Yna gwelais hwy'n cilio
      I'r wawr aur ar fryniau'r fro,
      Heibio i hen hud y bau-
      Heibio hun ei hunbennau.

IV

Neithiwyr gwenlloer ddisglair nofiai'r nefoedd,
Brudded a dwysed â breuddwyd oesoedd:
Pob rhyw hud a goludoedd-dorrai'n gân
Gywoeth o arian ar wig a thiroedd.
      Hyfryd uwch y cwm difri
      Casglai'r niwl delediw li
      Liw pebyll rhyw wersyll wawn
      Neu esgyll o farbl ysgawn.

Today the splendid princes
Under the stone sleep in their night;
But visit the buried brave
Their history and legends.
>   And from their fair quiet graves
>   Some magic flame at Strata Florida
>   And on the country breeze
>   A constant echo of their arms. "

Here was his talking
The happy magic, stilling the breezes
From the summit of the wooded hill - the host went
>   on
To a lovely longing remembering the brave.
>   Then I saw them retreating
>   To the golden dawn on the hills,
>   Past the old magic of the domain-
>   Past the sleep of the princes.

IV

Bright moonlit traveller floats in the heavens,
Sorrowful and solemn with dreams of time
All of some magic song of daybreak
A layer of silver on wood and pasture.
>   Lovely head of the solemn valley
>   Collecting the beautiful mist
>   The colour of tents around a gossamer camp
>   Or wings of light marble

Gwelwn drachefn rhyw anhrefn o wynros,
Gloywon wedd cerygl o winoedd ceirios
Ac ar waun ddiddig a rhos-gwelwn ynn
Ac aml dyddyn is eu cymyl diddos.
      Ac ar y pellter arian
      Lleuad oedd fel gelli dân,
      A'i hambr hud ar gwm a bron
      Dorrai'n ddewiniaeth dirion.

Yna mi welwn godi o'r moelydd
Eneidiau o'u hun, ar ddull dihenydd;
A llawer hen awenydd-gyrchai'r tir
O rug y gwyllt-dir a chreigiau gelltydd.
      Pob un yn cerdded wedyn
      Hyd ymyl swrth y deml syn,
      Ar wedd anhymig freuddwyd
      Addfwyn a lleddf, hen a llwyd.

A hwy yn cerdded rhwng ifanc wyrddail,
Drwy'r hwyr digymar, i oedfa'r adfail,
Tros y ffriw daeth gwynt miwail,-gan roi maith
Sidanog hoywiaith tros dwyn a gwiail.
      Deuai pob cysglyd awen
      O fedd oer canrifoedd hen;
      Tros ennyd torrai'u seiniau
      O'r mur breg yn furmur brau.

I see again some pink disorder,
Bright like cherry wine
And on peaceful moor mountain ash
And many a cottage on the sheltered lower edge.
    And in the silver distance
    The moon was like a flaming grove,
    And its mystic light on vale and ridge
    Looses its noble witchcraft.

Then I saw come from the hills
Souls of their own, in grand style;
And many old poet-haunts of the land
From the wild heather-land and rock cliffs.
    Each one walked then
    Up to the step of the temple,
    Into the dream
    Gentle and humble, old and grey.

And they walked between young saplings,
Through the incomparable night to the ruin,
Over the plain came the gentle wind, laying
Lively silk over home and branch.
    The muse came all sleepy
    From the cold grave centuries old;
    In a moment break the sounds
    From the wall's soft murmur.

Yna o'r tarthiau a'u haenau gwynion,
I hud yr oror, codai yr awron
Ddau yn dwyn nodau mwynion-prydferth oed
Rhyw oesau henoed o fflur a swynion.
  A than dangnef y nefoedd,
  Isel lais eu sisial oedd
  Megis peraidd, hafaidd hynt
  Soniarus awen hwyrwynt.

"Pa ryw waeth o phylodd pryd
Achle y mynach nychlyd,
Ac od yw cwsg wedi cau
Oed ei hirion baderau?
Ei Gred freg ai Ave gynt
Ai laswyr oll giliesynt;

Y Wyry a Phedr o'r tir ffodd
A'i Wyliau yntau welwodd:
Ar ei fin rhoed yr hinon
Amliwiog, flodeuog don;
Yntau frwd gorwynt y fro
Uwch ei wyrdd gysgle chwarddo.

"Ei hendrist neuadd gandryll
Gwynfannai gwae yn nwfn gwyll,
Ac yng nghôr ei sant Forwyn
Wele tyf dail Tafod Wyn.

Then from the vapours and their pale layers,
To magic's border, now arose
Two who bear the lovely notes
From some ancient age of Florida and spells.
     And under the roof of heaven,
     Their voice was a low whisper
     Such as the sweet, summery passage
     Tuneful and kindly muse.

"What would be better when waning
Than the monk's dusty refuge,
And if sleep has ended
An age of long prayer?
His holy creed and Ave
And rosary all flowing;

The Virgin and Peter fled from the land
And kept his holy day:
On its border given its due
Colourful floral wave;
The rushing storm
Above his green bed chamber.

"Her long-sad shattered hall
Shining in deep twilight gloom,
And in the choir of his Virgin saint
Behold the leaves of White Tongue.

"Er colli o'r gelli gân
Holl wŷr y mentyll arian,
Ni phaid rhos a phader rhydd
Eglwysi'r deiliog laswydd;
Ac yntau'r gosber ery
Eto ar fron coetir fry,
A chwardd ei glych rhydd a glas
Hyd eurlawnt y coed irlas.

Yn y twyni hyn tanom,
Yn y drwch dywarchen drom,
Hen unbennau a bonedd
Y syn fud mewn dison fedd;
Prifion rhyfel a helynt
Ewynnog, ysgythrog gynt,
Heddiw bedd di-gledd y glyn
Yn ddi-drwst gaeodd drostyn.

"Er edwi primas brodir
Ni thau neint â'u chwerthin hir;
Mwy dyred, fy ngem dirion,
I oed fry tan goed y fron;
Maer dewr bob un mewn hunell,
A marw yw gwŷr garw y gell;
O'u myned i drwm hunaw
I'w hedd hir, mi wn na ddaw
Angau i deml ieuengoed
Cariad gwin is gwridog goed.

"Despite the loss of the grove's song
All the men of the silver mantle,
The hill has no free priest
The church's leafy greenness;
And every evensong sounds
Again on the wooded slopes above,
The blue bells smile
And brighten the lush trees.

In the covering furrows,
In the thick heavy sod,
Old nobles and gentry
The mute in their quiet graves;
Leaders in war and wild tribulations
Once etched,
Today disarmed in the grave in the valley
Without noise closing over them.

"For thou keeps the first brothers
Not silent with their long laughter;
More desire, my gentle jewel,
To live under the wooded hill;
The brave men all in the ground,
And dead are the rough men of the cell;
From their coming to heavy soil
To the long peace, I know that comes
Death to the yew temple
Darling wine beneath rosy trees.

"Yno i'r deml o fanwydd
Dau o fwyn offeiriaid fydd;
O berthi'r haf ebyrth rhos
Dalant i Dduw y deilios;
Yn hud yr hwyr cân roi tro
I gangell fwsog yngo;
Ac oedfa eu serch gydfydd
A phader yr aber rydd;
A thrwy'r demel ddihelynt
Bydd nodau organau'r gwynt.

Yn y gwŷdd ni bydd ar gwêl;
Ond esmwyth seiniau dwsmel
Glyw y byd o'r ddirgel bau,
Ail dieithr drebl y duwiau;
Yno fyth ysbrydion fom,
A dryswaith o ddail drosom;
Ac erys seiniau'n cariad
Fel drysi ar lwyni'r wlad.

"Myfi a'm merch a bîau
A genir o berthi'r bau;
Ac oed wen y dadeni
Dramwyan hud drwom ni.
Er trigo nghudd tan hudd hwyr
Ein swyn fydd ar bob synnwyr."

Yma tawodd y llafar ar siarad
Maltae wynt blin yn llewin y lleuad;

66

"There, in the temple of brushwood
Two gentle priests;
From the summer offerings of moor hedges
Shall render to God the leaves;
The song of evening gives a turn
For chancel moss close by;
And the meeting joined together
The priest of the confluence;
And through the peaceful temple
Blow the notes of the wind organs.

In the wood all is quiet;
But the smooth sweet sounds
Heard in the world of the secret country,
Echo strangely the voice of gods;
There spirits come to lay
A blanket of leaves over us;
And there are still sounds of love
Like brambles on the rolling hills.

"I and my own daughter
Born of the hedged country;
And the white age of rebirth
Transmit magic through us.
For dwelling hidden until now
Our spell will charm every sense. "

Here the speaker held his speaking
As a bitter wind blew west of the moon;

A cherrynt o dawch irad-a threm bres
Yn araf wyres tros y dorf eurad.
Eithr ysgawn fwyn allwynin
Am ryw Ddafydd Gywydd Gwin
Yn nwsmel yr awel oedd
Ar y llennyrch a'r llynnoedd.

V

Gaeaf trwm ddaeth i'r cwm cau;
Ym mhenyd ei wynt, minnau
Dramwyais, tynnais at dan
Llety o'r eiry arian.

Cwrdd â llawen ŵr henoed
Yno ges, wrth dân o goed;
A diail y doedai o,
A'r rhewynt heibio'n rhuo:

"Bûm innau trwy'r tir mirain
Yng nghymun hud mud y main;
Yn y bau roedd lleisiau lleddf
Yn darllen brudiau oerlleddf,
Ail oriog sŵn galaru
O freuddwyd oer dyfroedd du;
Ac yno rhyw ŵr canwelw
Arhoai dan frigau'r derw;
Ei fantell chwyfiai wyntoedd
A'i wedd yn null Myrddin oedd,
Hithau y nos tros noeth nef
Ei gandryll aethog hendref.

68

A current of smoky fumes - and copper light
        climbing
Slowly over the gilded roof.
Beside a pale maid sorrowing
For some Dafydd the White Poet
In the gentle breeze that moved
On the glades and lakes.

V

Heavy winter came to the closeted valley;
In a breath of penance, I
Passed, I drew near to
Shelter from the silver snow

To meet a joyful elder man
There I was, by a woodfire
Unmatched it was
And the frosty passage roared:

"I myself went through noble land
In silent communion with the stones
In the country there were gentle voices
Reading chronicles of coldness,
Again a changing sound cries
From dreams of cold black waters;
And there some pale man
Under the branches of oak;
His robe stirring the wind
In the style and appearance of Merlin,
The night naked in the heavens
Her restless pale hall.

"A'i leddf air galwodd i fod
Oesau hen y freg Synod;
Ac ar hyn rhyw dri gŵr oedd
Yn tario ar y tiroedd
Mal dison ysbrydion brau
Cynnar haf y canrifau.

"Ar un roedd delw'r trinedd,
Gwisgiad dur ac esgud wedd;
A'i darian, fel ei diroedd,
Yn dolciog, ysgythrog oedd.
Y llall oedd mewn mantell wen,
Geined ag eiry gaenen;
A'i lwyd fin, cynefin oedd
A llaswyr y pell oesoedd.

"Y trydydd trwy'r lawnt rodiai
A'i drem oll fel mwynder Mai;
Ei hirwallt crych, eurwyllt, crog,
Donnai fel ffrwd adeiniog;
Ac ar ei fant ramant ros
I'w gariad wefus geirios.

Ar hyn y dewin a drodd,
A rhwydd i'r tri wŷr rhoddodd
Dair o glych diwair a glas
Wasgarai fiwsig eirias;
Ac wedyn y gwynt gododd,
A phawb o'r rhithiau a ffodd.

"And his least word to be called
Past ages of the Synod;
And this was about three men
Interred in these grounds
Like silent brittle ghosts
Of the early summer of the centuries.

"On one was depicted a warrior,
Wearing steel and looking bold;
And his shield, as his lands, was
Jagged, craggy.
The second was in a white robe,
Delicate of touch, under a snowy coating;
And with a grey edge, his home was
A rosary of distant ages.

"The third walked through the grass
And he gazed on all as bounteous May;
Her ridges rippling, golden, hanging,
Waving as a rushing stream;
And on her lip a romantic rose
For his love's cherry lip.

At this the magician turned,
And easily gave to the three men
Three pure bells of blue
Pealing a glowing music;
And then the wind rose,
And all of the illusions fled.

"O'u myned o'r cwm unig
I ryw oer, anghyffwrdd drig,
Da y gwn fod nwyd y gerdd
Yngo o hyd yn angerdd,-
Yn hud ail i sŵn deilios
Dan wynt pêr yn nyfnder nos;
A chân y clychau hynny
Yn y dud sant o hyd sy:
Canant ar lif drycinau,
Heibio i'r hen furddyn brau;
Canant am atgo einioes
Y byd aeth o wybod oes;
Ac yno rhydd cân y rhain
Alaw egyr Ein Plygain."

Ynar gŵr breg oer ei bryd,
Dawodd fel sŵn dyhewyd.

"When going from the lonely valley
To some cold, unfriendly dwelling,
Well I know the feeling of the poem
Always dense with passion, -
The magic becomes the sound of leaves
Under sweet wind in the depth of night;
A song of those bells
The saint found:
They sing on the turbid flow,
Past the fragile old ruin;
They sing about life
A world passed out of knowing;
And there sing these songs for others
A tune begins Our Matins. "

There the cold man of his time,
Held his peace like the sound of meditation.

R. S. THOMAS

Ystrad Fflur (Strata Florida)

I hardly knew him.
The place was old,
ruins of an ideal in chaste
minds. Rows of graves
signalled their disappointment.
Time, I said. Place, he replied,
not contradicting.

                    Had we found
what we sought, for him
somewhere, for me when
to listen to a mossed voice
beyond our dimensions?
Where are the twelve gates?
I wondered, looking at the low
archway through which we had come.
Had the years left us
only this one? Must masculine thoughts
once more be tonsured?

                    I am
a musician, the voice said.
I play on the bone keys in an audience's
absence. The light twitched,
as though at the blinking
of an immense eyelid; the foliage

rippled in shadowy applause.
We regarded one another,
neither wanting to be the first
to propose. Is every proposal
a renunciation? Was our return
mutual to where the machine offered
its accelerating alternatives
to the noon-day of the soul?

HARRI WEBB

Thanks in winter

The day that Eliot died I stood
By Dafydd's grave in Ystrad Fflur,
It was the depth of winter,
A day for an old man to die.
The dark memorial stone,
Chiselled in marble of Latin
And the soft intricate gold
Of the old language
Echoed the weather's colour,
A slate vault over Ffair Rhos,
Pontrhydfendigaid, Pumlumon,
The sheep-runs, the rough pasture
And the lonely whitewashed houses
Scattered like frost, the dwellings
Of country poets, last inheritors
To the prince of song who lies
Among princes, among ruins.
A pilgrim under the yew at Ystrad Fflur
I kept my vow, prayed for my country,
Cursed England, and came away.

And home to the gas fire and television
News. Caught between two languages,
Both dying, I thanked the long-dead
Minstrel of May and the newly silent

Voice of the bad weather, the precise
Accent of our own time, taught
To the disinherited, offering
Iron for gold.

RUTH BIDGOOD

At Strata Florida

This afternoon on the edge of autumn
our laughter feathers the quiet air
over tombs of princes. We idle
in an old nave, lightly approach
old altars. Our eyes, our hands
know fragments only; from these
the Abbey climbs and arches into the past.
We look up and find
only our own late August sky.

Ystrad Fflûr, your shadows fall
benevolently still on your ancient lands
and on us too, who touch your stones
not without homage. Take our laughter
on your consenting altars,
and to the centuries borne up
by your broken pillars, add
the light weight of an hour
at the end of summer.

MOELWYN MERCHANT

Dafydd lies at Ystrad Fflur

"Among the hills near the source of the Teifi, the few
remains of a once-flourishing Cistercian foundation;
Dafydd ap Gwilym lies buried somewhere within the
walls."   Guidebook entry

Within Teifi's floodland
rich acres and the distant
blue of hill ridges;
to the south, bog-grass and reed,
rusty red and the deep stain of peat,
the dreary beauty of Tregaron waste.

Inside the shadowed acre,
the walled enclosure of valid prayer,
secure in delving and planting,
pruning both rose and pen-quill,
in Strata-florida, the primrose way to paradise;
here are the Chronicles of Princes on vellum,
their bones also recorded and resting
in ordered rows outside the sanctuary.
"Dafydd ap Gwilym" we are told
"lies buried somewhere within the walls."

Somewhere; a casual mislaying of dust;
we have lost our brother,
the searching roots of that yew

perhaps marking the spot.
Stately requiescat,
sprinkled grace of asperging
leave this strong body
in dead soil smothered by day
and by night no striving.
It stirs in putrefaction,
clarifies in earth the witty struggle
of the flesh, the words stilled.

2

"Yes; Sundays at Llanbadarn
were spent with those of like mind;
I sat, knelt, half-knelt,
my face turned to the dark lass,
the nape of my neck to God."

Passion of the Mass, the flesh raised up,
a wanton look at the Host,
with blind adoration of the lady.

3

"Has anyone ever gone a-wooing
as I have? scouted love's trail,
ruttishly scurried along
the whole summer length of Cwcwll valley,
scoured the grounds of Gwgawn castle,

limped like a gosling in the meadow,
tramped the bound of Adail Heilin
with the lurch of a tired dog,
crouched above Ifor's court
like a monk cramped under a misericord,
impatient, panting for a glimpse
of sprightly Morfudd.

There's no hillock, no dull clump
in all the twistings of Nant-y-Gro
which hasn't tried my temper,
deprived of Ovid, my book of amours.

Easy to whisper gently, grasping
the dear quarry at Gwern-y-Talwrn
where I saw so still
my moon-girl dressed in chill black;
there, where man never sees
growing grass or bush in spring
we bedded under bare withies
on leaves bruised like Adam's trail.

A pitiful tale,
the weary, unsatisfied soul
following gracelessly the rough track
of the body's unparadised way."

4

Self-appointed laureate to Morfudd, writes:
      "By God-made-flesh I suffer bitterly,
      this teasing silence will be the death of me;
      life at its end will know great horror
      as death releases its cross-bow terror
      even this quick tongue forever silent
      as dull body obeys death's mute intent.
      Blessed Trinity, Mary Immaculate
      save me the pain of this deserved fate;

      Amen - no more ingenious rhymes."

5

"This ritual,
hazel sanctuary in the beech grove,
a holy place;
to-day's dawn set in hazel green,
the aubade of the dappled thrush
singing its Matins in the bright glade,
lyric gospel of love's messenger.

He had flow like a thought
from Carmarthen's quiet acres,
sent by my golden girl.

Wordy as licensed preacher
he flew to the arched hollow,
his wings draped with a chasuble
of flowers from the branches of Spring,
his cassock a wind-blown cloak
of plaited withies; and - I swear by God -
no baldachino here but heaven's gold vault.

Morfudd had commissioned him,
rhythmic music of Spring's child;
I listened to the tumbling words -
no clerk's stumbling mutter -
the Gospel declared to the faithful,
and saw the Host elevated,
a holy leaf on a high hill,
while within the sanctuary copse
the nightingale, trim, articulate,
chimed in her throat the sanctus-bell
as the sacrifice was raised
above the green glade,
worship in passion's chalice,
that pure song
in its birch sanctuary."

6

"Sheltering yesterday from the rain
under the green cloak of the birch,
best branches for a tent
I was waiting for a smile, like a foolish boy,
from my lass, a second Helen.

Suddenly I saw one
standing, outfacing me,
ugly, a man of foreboding.
I crossed myself, hoping
for the saints' grace.

      'Tell me - no with-holding -
      if you are a man, who are you?'

      'I am - no! no more questions -
      your own strange shadow;
      take in silence the stuff of my message.
      I have come on a merciful errand
      naked to your side
      to show you - a gem of precious knowledge!

-

      what you are, and what lies after.'

      'No generous gestures, foul nonentity;
      I am not what you think,
      hag's offspring, crookback of goatish kind.
      You are more like a miserable phantasm
      than a man of true feature:
      a herdsman wriggling in his plaid,
      a witch's broom on black stilts,
      shepherd of foul ghosts,
      bald, monkish scarecrow,
      herdsman playing childish games,
      a crammed heron grazing on bog-grass,
      opening wide its pinions,
      an idiot with holy palmer's face,

a blackfriar in a dirty cassock,
corpse wrapped in ashroud,
where have you hidden,
you scourings of the stable-yard?'

'Many a day stalking you,
and with a dangerous knowledge.'

'What hold have you on me,
pot-neck, more than the world well knows?
What do you know, devil's dung?
I have brought no shame to my neighbour,
I have killed with no subtle blow,
not gone hunting game with a sling,
I have offended no little one,
broken no vow,
coveted no stranger's wife.'

'If I revealed, by God,
to those who don't know your ways -
inevitable retribution -
indeed you would be hanged!'

'Then reveal nothing,
sew up your lips,
be secret'."

"Blood from the pure, pierced side,
        on Christ's tranquil Cross;
Divine breast, hold me,
sure spring of life, wash me!"

Dafydd meditates:
'They bound with bands your terrible innocence,
        pierced our ransom, nailed to a pine-tree,
        the cruel bonds enslaved the body
        borne by Mary to her deep sorrow.

Already on the cross the triumphant end
        flight from the grave
we see for our sakes; your saving passion,
        is it nothing to us, your pain?

Your feet drenched with blood, unseemly memory
your hands, dear God, for me pierced;
marks of death on the noble brow,
your temples thorn-wounded, your lips livid -
after this heavy, shameful death,
even the mob is forced to its knees.'

9

Anima Christi, sanctifica me
O holy, compassionate Trinity,
          single glory of prophecy,
fair soul of the slain Christ
cleanse me within like sweet linen.

Corpus Christi, salva me
Body of Christ, pity our boldness;
          flesh of the Eucharist
bring health to our souls -
as you live, O give me life.

O bone Iesu, exaudi me
Roll back the stone, save us;
Christ our light, dawn of each altar,
          our sacrifice of praise
receive without reproach.

Et ne permittas me separari a te
And give me a place, raise me,
to your right hand, Prince of the world;
hedge me about, keep me safe,
that I may praise in glory without end.

Amen
And take me at last to that fair kingdom -
          an obedient servant -
to that noble country, fair heritage,
God's marriage feast and lordly rule.

10

"Teifi's nightingale is silenced!"

The passion of the Eucharist has bound
altar and tree, leaf thrusting
like salmon, and a man
like leaf, like salmon, torque twisting,
leaping up to his God.

And now
a seemly stillness regiments
the ruins of Ystrad Fflur
and at the north flank, near the altar,
the Princes of Deheubarth, skull by shank-bone
mingled with monks and aboots;
the dust casually scattered,
Dafydd lies buried somewhere,
that busy flesh
          unnaturally silent.

GILLIAN CLARKE

At Ystrad Fflur

No way of flowers at this late season.
        Only a river blossoming on stone
        and the mountain ash in fruit.

All rivers are young in these wooded hills
        where the abbey watches and the young Teifi
        counts her rosary on stones.

I cross by a simple bridge constructed
        of three slim trees. Two lie across. The third
        is a broken balustrade.

The sun is warm after rain on the red
        pelt of the slope, fragmentary through trees
        like torches in the dark.

They have been here before me and have seen
        the sun's lunulae in the profound
        quietness of water.

The Teifi is in full flood and rich
        with metals: a torc in a brown pool
        gleaming for centuries.

I am spellbound in a place of spells. Cloud
        changes gold to stone as their circled bones
        dissolve in risen corn.

The river races for the south too full
        of summer rain for safety, spilt water
        whitening low-lying fields.

From oak and birchwoods through the turning trees
        where leaf and hour and century fall
        seasonally, desire runs

Like sparks in stubble through memory
        of the place, and a yellow mustard field
        is a sheet of flame in the heart.

Dyddgu replies to Dafydd

All year in open places, underneath
       the frescoed forest ceiling,
       we have made ceremony
       out of this seasonal love.

Dividing the lead-shade as divers white
       in green pools we rose to dry
       islands of golden sun. Then
       love seemed generosity.

Original sin I whitened from your
       mind, my colours influenced
       your flesh, as sun on the floor
       and warm furniture of a church.

So did our season bloom in mild weather,
       reflected gold like butter
       under chins, repeatedly
       unfolding to its clock of seed.

Autumn, our forest room is growing cold.
       I wait, shivering, feeling a
       dropping sun, a coming dark,
       your heart changing the subject.

The season coughs as it falls, like a coal;
       the trees ache. The forest falls
       to ruin, a roofless minster
       where only two still worship.

Love still, like sun, a vestment, celebrates,
        its warmth about our shoulders.
        I dread the day when Dyddgu's once
        loved name becomes a common cloak.

Your touch is not so light. I grow heavy.
        I wait too long, grow anxious,
        note your changing gestures, fear
        desire's alteration.

The winter stars are flying and the owls
        sing. You are packing your songs
        in a sack, narrowing your
        words, as you stare at the road.

The feet of young men beat, somewhere far off
        on the mountain. I would women
        had roads to tread in winter
        and other lovers waiting.

A raging rose all summer falls to snow,
        keeps its continuance in
        frozen soil. I must be patient
        for the breaking of the crust.

I must be patient that you will return
        when the wind whitens the tender
        underbelly of the March grass
        thick as pillows under the oaks.

CAROLINE GILL

1st May: Red Kite at Strata Florida

How many feet have entered through the arch?
How many lines have issued from the pen?
How many pilgrim souls have shone a torch
on stony hearts through centuries of rain?

And yet the sun still shines upon the earth
and poetry seeps out from moss and tile.
A woman kneels upon an ancient hearth
to gather dew: cupped hands become a bowl.

The turf unfurls like wool: the sheep are still
when all at once a comet floods the sky
with scarlet light, and mountains disappear
beneath a blaze of fire. A flash of steel
soars overhead in loops of ecstasy,
as pounding wings become a distant whirr.

BYRON BEYNON

Ystrad Fflur

"prydydd à'i gywydd fel gwin"[1]

The third week of an indifferent July
where a patient landscape waits
for summer's enlightenment to arrive,
no sunshine caught
the spell of afternoon
only the sound of distant
sheep and the craft of tailwind
stirring a listening atmosphere
carrying the speech of time.
A brutal wonder
as wings of prey motioned,
caught momentarily riding
their natural geometry above a silent Yew;
the flesh of words bonding
in a family of rhymes,
the lover, the friend,
a sudden calling of birds
on a vaulted air of praise.

---

[1] [a poet and his poem like wine]

GWYNETH LEWIS

Ystrad Fflur

Pan fydda i farw, taenwch fy llwch,
Os gwelwch yn dda, yn Ystrad Fflur.
Dychmygodd Taliesin ei hun
Yn gell. Rwy'n gweld y mynaich
Yn grwm wrth gopïo DNA
Ein dychymyg yn Strata Florida.
Bryd hynny, bydd y ddraenen wen yn fwg
O goelcerth y perthi, byddaf falch
Fel mwyalchen. Gwisgaf y gwynt, fy nghorff
Ac, mewn munud, daw awel lem
O'r mynydd gan iasu'r glaswellt yn emau byw.

Comisiynwyd gan Cadw

96

Strata Florida

Soil is the dead
Of all ages. Pass
Through this door
Into Christ, the expanding
Universe. Dimension:
Wonder. Uplands bare,
Riches below. Through
This door, be proud
As a blackbird,
Where the humble fern
Blossomed to stone,
Then back again. This
Door. Find your own elsewhere.
Now. The future. Then. Then now.

Commissioned by Cadw

Part 2

MARTIN LOCOCK

Scribe and scripture

I smooth the soft vellum
    Sunlight warms the cloister
I mark the lines with pin pricks
    My calloused feet are cold
I mix the bitter ink
    Axes fall in distant woodland
I choose a goose quill
    A yeasty scent blows from the frater
I cut the nib to an edge
    The others bend over their desks
And I begin to write
    "To the Glory of God . . . "

Gorffwysfa
(Resting place for Dafydd ap Gwilym)

Between high hill and the plain
Between forest and meadow
Between Glasffrwd and Teifi

Between this world and the next
Between the flesh and spirit
Between my birth and rebirth

Within this most holy ground
Beneath venerable yew
Cradled by old stones I rest

Gorffwysfa Dafydd ap Gwilym

Rhwng mynydd ac ystrad
Rhwng coed glas a dolydd
Rhwng Glasffrwd a Theifi

Rhwng y byd hwn a'r nesaf
Rhwng y cnawd ac ysbryd
Rhwng geni ac aileni

Yn y lle mwyaf sanctaidd hwn
Dan ywen hen a pharchus
Ymhlith hen gerrig arhosaf

KATHY MILES

The Creed of Cataloguing

'Perhaps the blood of a monk,' he says
as he lays down the manuscript
with loving, white-gloved fingers.
We peer enthralled at the stained page
imagine Brother Cadwgan
kneeling to pray in the cloister.
The swift treason of a knife.

He catalogues the monks:
Brother Anian's neat letters
Rhydderch ab Ieuan's distinctive hand.
No novice to this task, he searches
for provenance, skims through the rules
of his order, turning hierarchies
to numbers, logical, precise.

He runs his fingers over the spine,
tooled leather, endbands,
codices gathered into quires.
He is a text-seeker, eager
to sink himself into litany or missal,
the musky echo of flesh,
lampblack and salts of old ink.

He pictures five scribes
working with aching backs
in the dim scriptorium.
Transcribing annals, copying
breviary or psalm,
laying gold leaf on a ground of gesso,
casing psalters in soft chemise.

And the poet, too,
buried by the abbey grounds
with his immaculate verses
still singing *cywyddau* in his head.
He too is classified, codified,
as he lies in the valley of flowers
under a twisted girdle of yew.

CAROL MANWELL

Scriptorium

What we were after there, in the horn and vellum,
as we scraped parchment and cut horns for ink,
was to clear a field our scholar monks could plough
with their sharp quills, sowing a crop
seeds black as peppercorns or elderberries
to be harvested and stored in libraries.

SUE MOULES

The Pilgrim

"All of us are pilgrims in a sense, moving through our lives, looking for something." Glenn Morris

The pilgrim walks across the sky,
touches stars with his stick.
He is wood and wool and spirit,
walks the up and down roads
seeking his god.

The weather has taken its toll,
reduced him to the barren of winter tree,
stubble of wool . His clothes worn out;
still he climbs,
reaches for the star beyond.

The Taliesin Stone

The artist takes the poet's words
and like the blackbird breaks them
on stones, on river boulders.
Fragments of mother of pearl,
white and gold,
tactile swirls of water.

Red and blue mosaics
stop and start sentences,
like the inks the monks made
to copy the ancient stories
with their quills on vellum.

Skilled artists they
filled historiated letters
with miniatures of themselves,
bearded faces,
cobalt blue infill
and gold leaf. Such expense,
finery for the glory of God.

The Taliesin Stone : a sculpture by Rob Turner using the words of Gwyneth Lewis'poem for Ystrad Ffur (p. 97)

ANTHONY KENDREW

Strata Florida

I went notebook in hand
but too cold to unglove
to command the fingers
hold the pen
to execute the illuminations
the sacred demands of us
meanwhile the mind
appalled at the ice-caked mud
and crisp white grass
was obsessing over soup
and more intrigued
by the tapping of a bird in the yew tree
than expressing the appropriate awe
at the possibility that
here lies Dafydd ap Gwilym
even though his dancing limbs
his breezy gait
the harp
one or two of the racier poems
the sheer enviable sexiness
of the man
were apparent
so it was the layers
the layers
that saved the morning
from banality

layers of dirt
layers of sky and landscape
layers of lives
here where the sloping fields
enclose and embrace the time
and time contracts
or disappears
enough for us
to stop
and stare

AMANDA PICKERING

Cyfeillgarwch (friendship)

Inseparable, they met
in Ysgol Bont
Huw the boy born lame
with sunshine in his soul
and his shy friend Ian.

Their bond as golden as the veins
at Dolaucothi mine
as Huw, the child with steel rods
strapped to his legs
grew into the man with backbone.

He joked back at life,
his laughter fizzing and bubbling
like a mountain stream,
Huw Siop as he was known.

Ian married his Myfanwy.
They were there through Huw's last illness
a pair of sentinel swans
their arms through his
keeping him afloat.

They would lift him into the car
take him on outings,
to appointments in London

and pushed for a place
where he could live,
not cloistered in a nursing home
but in his own way.

And they stayed with him
through the long nights
until his breath loosened
like thistle-down and softly
floated away.

Huw is buried in the *cwm*
beside his mother and father
at Ystrad Fflur,
where Welsh poppies shine
sun yellow through a silver blur of rain.

MARY OVERTON

Benediction

The boy leans on the great stone ribs, rubbing his shin,
kicked again as the cattle jostled through the arch
drawn by the scent of hay laid in the stalls within
the shelter of the old scriptorium, its hard
earth floor bracken-bedded. He ties each hungry beast,
avoids Nell's hooves that try to catch him one more blow,
trims the lamp, shakes up his raggy bed and lies to sleep,
thinks of his home, kneels up, asks God to grant repose.

Through a high ruined transom the moon illumines ropes
of heavy cobwebs swinging in the air. Disturbed,
the boy sits up. A hooded form, face masked by folds
of grey, moves among the cows, strokes one, speaks quiet words
and bends to gentle milk into a leathern pail
then signs a blessing over her. The boy now sleeps;
at dawn he milks, stripping the full udders, all save
one. For Nell has no milk to give, but lets him feel,
and nuzzles his shoulder. Her feet stay still, and now
across his mind's eye flits an image in a cowl.

JOSIE SMITH

Strata Florida

Nine yew trees guard this holy place
surrounded by the Cambrian hills
bounded by water from the Teifi pools
a refuge from this world of haste
where pilgrims pause to hear the sounds
of chanting monks, of praise and prayer,
drink healing water from the grail where
once the sacred blood flowed from His wounds.
Deheubarth's Prince, Yr Arglwydd Rhys
created here this place of light
where sky and earth speak of the might
of God, and bring the gift of peace,
and sleeping now, the whitened bones
of princes lie beneath their stones.

Contributors

BYRON BEYNON

Byron Beynon lives in Swansea. His work has appeared in several publications including *The Independent*, *Agenda*, *Poetry Wales*, *Poetry Ireland*, *Chicago Poetry Review* and *London Magazine*. Recent collections include *Cuffs* (Rack Press), *Nocturne in Blue* and *Human Shores* (both from Lapwing Publications, Belfast). A Pushcart Prize nominee. He has lectured on Poetry & The Mirror of Art as part of the Dylan Thomas Festival, at the Glynn Vivian Art Gallery. A series of ten poems appeared in the anthology *Evan Walters: Moments of Vision* (Seren Books).

RUTH BIDGOOD (b. 1922)

Ruth Bidgood was born near Neath in south Wales and studied at Oxford. After her marriage she lived in Surrey working as a publishing editor, before moving to Abergwesyn in Powys in the 1970s. She has published several collections of poems including *New and Selected Poems* (2004) and *Above the Forests* (2012).

GILLIAN CLARKE (b. 1937)

Gillian Clarke, National Poet for Wales since 2008, was born in Cardiff and lives in Ceredigion. Her work is widely studied for GCSE and A Level. She is President of Tŷ Newydd, the Welsh Writers Centre which she co-founded in 1990. She has published ten collections of poems and a book of prose, *At the Source*. Her latest poetry collection, *Ice*, was shortlisted for the T S Eliot Award, 2012. In 2010 she was awarded the Queen's Gold Medal for Poetry.

115

LINDEN FLETCHER
Rooted in farming, Christian faith, and arts education, especially music, Linden Fletcher now lives near Lampeter and is a member of a local art group.

CAROLINE GILL
Caroline Gill's poetry chapbook, *The Holy Place*, co-authored with John Dotson, was published by The Seventh Quarry (Swansea) and Cross-Cultural Communications (New York). Caroline won the international Petra Kenney Poetry Competition (General Section) in 2007. Her poems have been published widely in the UK and beyond. Caroline is married to David Gill, an archaeologist. Website www.carolinegillpoetry.com

EDWIN STANLEY JAMES
Edwin Stanley James was an English and Welsh language poet active in the 1940s, publishing *Tro ar Fyd*, *Short Measures* and *The Statue and other Poems*.

DAFYDD JOHNSTON (b. 1955)
Dafydd Johnston was born in East Yorkshire. He is a specialist on medieval Welsh poetry, and is Director of the University of Wales Centre for Advanced Welsh and Celtic Studies in Aberystwyth. He has published a number of bilingual texts, including *Iolo Goch: Poems* (Gomer, 1993) and *Medieval Welsh Erotic Poetry* (Tafol, 1991).

T. GWYNN JONES (1871-1949)

Thomas Jones was born in Betws-yn-Rhos, Denbighshire; he had a varied career as an editor and publisher, working at the National Library of Wales and becoming Professor in Celtic Studies at Aberystwyth University. He wrote extensively in Welsh, including poetry, drama and academic studies.

ANTHONY KENDREW

Anthony Kendrew likes to explore connections between the inner and outer landscapes - the inspiration for much of his writing. He lives and works in a remote and beautiful part of Northern California and is currently doing a Creative Writing MA at the University of Wales Trinity Saint David in Lampeter.

GWYNETH LEWIS (b. 1959)

Gwyneth Lewis was born in Cardiff and has worked as a journalist and broadcaster. She was National Poet of Wales in 2005. She writes poetry in English and Welsh. Her most recent collection is Sparrow Tree (Bloodaxe,. 2011).

MARTIN LOCOCK (b. 1962)

Martin Locock was born in Bath, Somerset, and has worked as a professional archaeologist in Wales from 1991-2002; since then he has been a project manager at the National Library of Wales and University of Wales Trinity Saint David. He has published three collections of poetry through his publishing firm, Carreg Ffylfan Press, the latest being *Removals*.

CAROL MANWELL
Carol Manwell is a part-time General Practitioner and a poet. She was born in Northern Ireland just after the war, spent her early years in the Southern Sudan, and is now smallholder in Wales.

MOELWYN MERCHANT (1913-1997)
Moelwyn Merchant was born in Port Talbot. He taught English Literature at Cardiff and Exeter Universities, and was also an Anglican minister, novelist and sculptor.

KATHY MILES
Kathy Miles was born in Liverpool and now works in Lampeter as Outreach Services Librarian at the University of Wales, Trinity Saint David. She has contributed to numerous anthologies and poetry magazines, and has published three books: *The Rocking Stone, The Third Day: Landscape and the Word,* and *The Shadow House.* She loves gardening, animals and writing, and lives near to the sea with a partner and a stroppy cat.

SUE MOULES
Sue Moules is a founder member of the Lampeter Writers' Workshop. Her poems have appeared in many magazines and anthologies. She has published three individual collections, the most recent being *The Earth Singing* (Lapwing 2010).

AMANDA PICKERING
Amanda has lived in Wales for many years. She is a nurse and works at the community hospital in Tregaron. She is a poet and artist.

JOSIE SMITH (b. 1947)

Josie Smith was born in London and has lived in Wales since 1973. She was awarded an M.A. in Creative and Scriptwriting at University of Wales, Lampeter in 2007. Josie has had work broadcast by BBC Wales Radio and TV, had articles published in several journals, including the international publication *Darshan magazine*. Josie has three grown children, two grandchildren, has run a Health Food Shop for 40 years and is a meditation teacher. She has written a film script, several short-stories and a novel, and is currently working on a series of fourteen sonnets. Josie enjoys walking in the Welsh countryside and is inspired by all life and nature.

R. S. THOMAS (1913-2000)

R. S. Thomas was an Anglican clergyman who served a range of rural Welsh parishes. His engagement with Welsh nationalism, culture and history proved a rich source of inspiration.

SCOTT WABY

Scott Waby is head of the Digitisation Unit at the National Library of Wales in Aberystwyth and a photographer.

HARRI WEBB (1920-1994)

Harri Webb was born in Swansea; he spent much of his career as a librarian in the South Wales valleys.

HEDD WYN (1887-1917)

Ellis Humphrey Evans was born in Trawsfynydd and worked on the family farm until enlisting in the army.

He had established a reputation as a Welsh language poet under the bardic name *Hedd Wyn*, and he was awarded the National Eisteddfod chair for his poem 'Yr Arwr' shortly after his death at Passchandaele.

Acknowledgments

The text and translations of the poems by Dafydd ap Gwilym, Gruffudd Grug, Guto'r Glyn and Dafydd Nanmor appear courtesy of Dafydd Johnston.

T. Gwynn Jones 'Ystrad Fflur' appears courtesy of Mrs Nonn Davies.

R. S. Thomas 'Ystrad Fflur' appears courtesy of Gwydion Thomas.

Harri Webb 'Thanks in Winter' appears courtesy of Meic Stephens.

Moelwyn Merchant 'Dafydd lies at Ystrad Fflur' appears courtesy of Paul Merchant.

The editor is grateful for the assistance of the staff of Bangor University, the National Library of Wales and Gwasg Gomer in locating rights holders.

The following poems were published previously:

Dafydd ap Gwilym 'Mis Mai a Mis Tachwedd', from *www.dafyddapgwilym.net*

Gruffudd Gryg 'I'r ywen uwchben bedd Dafydd ap Gwilywm', from Barry J. Lewis and Eurig Salisbury (eds.) *Gwaith Gruffudd Gryg* (Canolfan Uwchefrydiau Cymreig a Cheltaidd Prifysgol Cymru, Aberystwyth 2010)

Guto'r Glyn 'Salwch yr Abad Rhys ap Dafydd o Ystrad-fflur', from *www.gutorglyn.net*

T. Gwynn Jones 'Ystrad Fflur' from *Caniadau* (Hughes a'i fab, Wrecsam, 1934). Translation by Edwin Stanley James published in *Wales* **5 vii** (1945)

Hedd Wyn 'Ystrad Fflur', from *Cerddi'r Bugail* (Hughes a'i fab, Wrecsam, 1918)

R. S. Thomas 'Ystrad Ffliur (Strata Florida), from *Experimenting with an Amen* (Seren, Bridgend, 1986) and also in *Collected Poems 1945-1990* (Phoenix, 2000)

Harri Webb 'Thanks in winter', from *The Green Desert* (Gwasg Gomer, Llandysul, 1969), and also in *Looking up England's arsehole* (ed. Meic Stephens), Y Lolfa, Talybont (2000)

Ruth Bidgood 'At Strata Florida', from *Not Without Homage* (C. Davies (Publishers) Ltd, 1975), and also in *New and Selected Poems* (Seren, Bridgend, 2004)

Moelwyn Merchant 'Dafydd lies at Ystrad Fflur', from *Breaking the Code* (Gwasg Gomer, 1975)

Gillian Clarke 'At Ystrad Fflur', 'Dyddgu replies to Dafydd', from *The Sundial* (Gwasg Gomer, Llandysul, 1978) and also in *Collected Poems* (Carcanet, Manchester, 1997).

Caroline Gill '1st May: Red Kite at Strata Florida', from *The Seventh Quarry* **10** (Summer 2009) and *The Holy Place* ('Poet to Poet' chapbook by John Dotson and Caroline Gill, published by The Seventh Quarry Press, Swansea, in conjunction with Cross-Cultural Communications, New York, 2012)

Byron Beynon 'Ystrad Fflur', from *Nocturne in Blue* (Lapwing Publications, Belfast, 2009).

Gwyneth Lewis 'Strata Florida, from *Heritage in Wales* **49** (2011) and 'Ystrad Fflur' from *Etifeddiaeth y Cymry* **49** (2011)

Martin Locock 'Scribe and scripture', 'Gorffwysfa (Resting place for Dafydd ap Gwilym)' from *Removals* (Carreg Ffylfan Press, Ammanford, 2012)